Busy Beach

HOUGHTON MIFFLIN   BOSTON

The beach is a busy place,
even when it is not crowded
with people.

You can see bugs buzzing in
the sun.

1

Little fish swim in tide pools.
Snails are on the rocks.

Crabs crawl through the
seaweed.

One seagull has a fish, but
the other seagulls like to eat
fish too!